I Felt No Sorrow This Was War

Gordon Heynes

Edition 1.0

For Anthea

Forward

My grandfather Gordon Henry Heynes lived a fairly conventional life. Born in 1904, the youngest of four children, he was raised in the small Shropshire town of Craven Arms. As a young man he enjoyed riding his motorcycle through the countryside and playing cricket for the local team. He forged a career with Lloyds bank, and through his work re-located to the city of Gloucester where, in 1935, he married fellow bank worker, Muriel Colwell.

Gordon and Muriel bought a solid red-brick house on the edge of the city and were both to live there for the rest of their days. They had two children, daughter Anthea (my mother), born at the start of World War II, and son Ian, born soon after the war.

Gordon died in 1982, on my eighteenth birthday, and left me happy memories of a kindly old man who enjoyed ornithology and painting.

But for four years his life was far removed from homelife, bank work, and tranquil hobbies. His service in the Royal Armoured Corps during World War II saw him experience the horrors of battlefield combat first-hand. He fought in the Burma Campaign against the invading Japanese forces, in time being seriously injured by shrapnel from a bomb that killed many of those around him.

Some time after his return to civilian life, Gordon wrote of his wartime experiences in a one-off book for his family and friends to read. He wrote with an appealing matter-of-fact style that truly brought home the reality of his story to the reader. My brother Gary and I felt that our grandfather's words were deserving of a wider audience, and so we prepared this book from his original manuscript. 7945642 Trooper G H Heynes didn't give his book a title; the one that we chose is a poignant quote from his text that we feel is appropriate.

Neal Bircher

1. Training in England

Thursday 16th October 1941

My brother-in-law Arthur called for me in his car and took me to catch the 8 o'clock train to Bristol. I could not face a farewell from Muriel and Anthea, 22 months old, on a station platform.

The journey to Bristol was slow and the weather dull and I was feeling far from bright, but the step had been taken and there was no turning back.

A month before I had gone to the recruiting centre at Gloucester and there they had asked what I wished to join. I suggested the Glosters, but they said there were no vacancies. They spent some time looking up the latest circulars and discovered that the following month there would be two vacancies in the Royal Armoured Corps. The fact that in my younger days I had spent much time and money on motorcycles and had owned one of the early Austin Sevens which I used to decarbonise myself seemed to be ample proof that I was just the sort of person to fit into the crew of the modern fighting vehicle known as a tank.

This was why I found myself making the journey to Wool to join the 52nd Training Regiment, Royal Armoured Corps at Bovington.

I changed at Bristol, bought a paper and took the train to Wareham. The main news in the paper was that there had been a big raid over Germany and we had lost over 10% of our planes and we were always being told that 4% was the most we could afford and carry on bombing. This news did not help to brighten up the day.

We reached Wareham and I changed again. The platform was deserted except for one man, and we got talking and discovered that we were both bound for the same place also that we were both in Lloyds Bank. His name was Radford and from then on we were together for a long time.

The London train came in and we joined it for the short journey to Wool. We alighted and with twenty-odd others set off for the three-mile trek to Camp. What a motley crowd, half were over thirty-five and the others under twenty.

When we reached camp we handed in our papers, then we were issued with mugs, knives, forks and spoons and given a meal, and for war time it was jolly good. After the meal we were issued with blankets and taken to an old army hut which was to be ours for the next six weeks, the period of our initial training.

There were thirty of us in our hut, all the older ones in the intake. Some of them were old soldiers who had served their time in India and a more foul lot would have been hard to find. There was another Lloyds Bank chap, he was very happy because he had got away from his wife, a peculiar fellow.

Lights out at 10.15 so at 9.30 we started making up our beds, blankets only, no sheets, not very comfortable.

The first few days were spent being kitted out. This meant marching from one store to another, queuing up and waiting your turn. Also, we had medical examinations and inoculations.

After a week we looked like soldiers, our civilian clothes had been sent home and this included our pyjamas, so from then one slept in our pants (long) and vests.

Training started but only drill and PT. It seemed that the most important thing was to have a shine on your boots, like glass. Every night we spent hours on these boots and nearly as long on the brasses. I was fortunate in that my great coat had bone buttons and I was never told to change them.

The first six weeks went by slowly but the drill and open-air life was good for me and I was feeling very fit. We had our passing out parade and then leave.

Back from leave we had less drill and started driving lorries. Some of the chaps had never driven so when you were driving in convoy it paid to keep well away from the vehicle in front as anything could happen. One day we were going up a hill when the driver in front instead of changing into bottom changed into reverse and came charging back. Fortunately his instructor managed to grab the hand brake and pull up just short of my lorry.

After a few weeks on lorries we started on Bren Carriers. I found them easy to manage on open country but on roads it was very easy to skid especially if it had been raining.

Next we were introduced to tanks, no steering wheel, just two sticks, it took time to adjust yourself to this. In time you began to feel yourself at home when you were transferred to another tank, generally a bigger one. We finished up on Churchills, 50 tonnes and 500 HP engines. From the turret of this mighty tank poked out the gun, a miserable little two pounder. In those days it looked absurd - just imagine what the present-day soldier would think of it.

We spent much time driving over the moors, it was very pleasant on fine days, out past Lawrence's cottage up the hill. You found that when you were driving downhill the tank overtook the engine and you had reverse steering, very disconcerting.

When there was snow and slush about you prayed that nothing would go wrong which would necessitate getting out and working on the tracks sometimes with mud a foot deep.

After some weeks of this we moved to Lulworth for a gunnery course. The camp there was in a wood and we were in old army huts, it was a wet and cold period and everything was wet including our blankets.

The entrance to the camp looked out over the sea and what a grim place it looked. At night you could see the searchlights on the French coast and when there was a raid on the bomb burst showed up clearly. One night I was on guard at the main entrance, an old regular was on with me and we each had a sentry box. It was bitterly cold and our hands were frozen and he told me that he remembered an old trick. We jabbed our bayonets into the wood of the sentry box so that the rifles were at the right angles and just above our shoulders. We spent the rest of the period with our rifles at shoulder arms but with our hands in our pockets.

After a few weeks at Lulworth we returned to Bovington for more tank training.

One night we were called out to stand to, rifles were issued with ammunition and we thought it was just a practice alert but before long we heard aircraft overhead and, soon after, bombs going off a few miles away. The Germans were bombing a fighter station, and later-on we knew why: it was the day the three German battleships were breaking out of Brest.

About this time it was the anniversary of the battle in the First World War when tanks were first used and we were given a special meal. I was detailed to do fatigues in the cookhouse so missed my meal in the dining hall but was allowed to help myself later. There was roast beef, Yorkshire pudding etc. I have always loved Yorkshire pudding and here was my big chance. I covered the plate with it before piling on the meat, roast potatoes and sprouts. I had had enough; I could not manage the sweet.

Early in March I was sent back to Lulworth for an advanced course on tank gunnery. The weather was good, the trees were coming into bud, the birds were singing, and I was looking forward to the next few months. We were divided into classes of five, in my class three were under twenty, the fourth was twenty-one and I was thirty-eight. However, all was going well until a fortnight later when my name appeared in Regimental Orders for drafting overseas.

Back to Bovington, where we spent three weeks on kit inspections and the issue of tropical kit. The last item we received was a revolver, so we knew it was the real thing.

We paraded on Sunday morning 12th April 1942. The regimental band led us round the parade ground then turned right and we turned left and marched to Wool station. From there we travelled to Southampton, which looked in a sorry state from the bombing they had had.

We then headed North, right up through the centre of England. It was a perfect day, the countryside looked so lovely, fresh green showing everywhere and the larks were singing overhead.

In the dead of night we reached Edinburgh and continued on to Glasgow. Our carriage was taken off the train and we finished at the docks. At eight o'clock we were given a meal and went onboard the boat.

2. Journey to India

It was the Orbita, a Pacific Steam Navigation boat which in peace time carried two hundred passengers to South America. In the first war she was used as a troop ship and was being used again carrying five thousand troops a trip.

We were the first troops to go on board, there were one hundred and twenty in our draft and we imagined there would be plenty of room but by the time we had filled up it was pretty crowded.

Being trained in gunnery a number of us were put in charge of the four Orlikon anti-aircraft guns. These were in turrets, one each side of the bridge and two at the rear of the boat. We were to be on duty in the turrets two hours in twelve throughout the voyage. In the daytime it was quite pleasant but at night the time dragged and you were always glad when it was over.

Berthed next to us was the American Aircraft Carrier, WASP. Her flight deck towered above us, we were only thirteen tons. A few months later she came to a sticky end at the hands of the Japs in the Pacific.

In the afternoon of Wednesday 15th April 1942 we slipped quietly down the Clyde. The shipyards were busy, there was a cruiser with its bridge blown off and no end of ships with damage of some kind or other.

The journey out to sea was wonderful, the many islands looked so green against the blue sea and the sun was sinking in the West in a cloudless sky.

Radford and I were on duty on the Orlikon on the starboard side of the bridge at 10 o'clock, it was very dark and we could just see the outline of the ships near us, there was one big one which kept coming quite close and I heard the Captain say to the second officer "that big fellow will be into us soon". When we were next on duty the next day all was sorted out and we could see the whole of the convoy as we zigzagged along. There were five troop ships and about a dozen cargo boats, we were in the front line of the ships, the second from the left and on the extreme right was the Cape Town Castle. There were two cruisers behind us and a special ack-ack ship which carried a Walrus seaplane which had to be catapulted off and when returning from a flight was winched up from the sea. Away in the distance, ahead and on both sides was a screen of about twenty destroyers and frigates.

We settled down to the routine although life was hard, only salt water to wash in and the food was poor. One day a week after breakfast we were given a tin of corned beef and some biscuits and this had to last the rest of the day, this was the one day we looked forward to. For the first five days we were not allowed to undress at night and trying to sleep in a hammock slung above the tables in the mess room where the air was foul and stagnant was very difficult. Radford and I decided it would be better on deck, so we found a spot on the top deck between the funnels. Here we remained for some time but when we reached warmer climes we were kicked off as the top deck was for officers only.

One morning we awoke to find that our screen of destroyers had left us leaving behind two frigates which sailed along, one on each side of the convoy. The job of the destroyers had been done, they had seen us safely across the Atlantic and left to join up with another convoy going the other way.

I found it very interesting when we were hundreds of miles from the nearest land to see little groups of stormy petrels, known as Mother Carey's chickens, flying along between the waves, I never saw any of them land.

Occasionally one of our flying boats flew round us and one night, when Radford and I were on duty, a plane approached and flew over us. I got into the Orlikon harness and Radford stood by to reload. We had been told never to fire on a plane until the ack-ack ship opened up, and that one of our own planes would never fly over the convoy, it was quite dark and I kept my sights on the plane which I could just see. Then the ack-ack ship sent up a Verey light which lit up everything. Nothing happened, the plane flew away. It must have been one of ours probably checking up on the convoy but in the darkness getting a bit out of position.

One morning the second officer on the bridge was a bit talkative and told us that there had been a warning of submarines in the night but the convoy had been able to alter course in time.

The night before we reached Freetown we saw a ship approaching with lights full on, it was heading straight for the middle of the convoy. We wondered what on earth would happen, it came nearer and nearer and then all the ships in the convoy switched on their navigation lights and it sailed right through the middle of us. One of our frigates followed it and when, no doubt, satisfied that it was neutral it was allowed to sail on.

Next day, after a fortnight at sea we saw land ahead and some hours later entered the mouth of the river at Freetown. How lovely and green it all looked, we hoped to be allowed to go on shore but we were told that there was a lot of malaria about so we remained on board for the five days we remained there. The temperature was very high and on the second day it got even higher and we finished up with a terrific thunderstorm. The rain came down in sheets and the men, myself included, dashed up on deck naked, armed with a tablet of soap and had a lovely wash down. How lovely it was to be able to use fresh water after using salt water for a fortnight.

We sailed from Freetown and started our voyage to the Cape. In addition to the cruisers we were now joined by a battleship, it was either the Royal Sovereign or the Resolution.

For some time we travelled quite close to the land and it was nice to see the hills and mountains.

We then lost sight of land and I found my interest taken up in watching the flying fish, the porpoise and later on the albatrosses. What a wonderful sight they were, ten feet wingspan, just gliding round and rarely flapping their wings.

We now crossed the Equator and the heat below deck was unbearable. Every evening we watched the sun go down, the lower rim just touched the horizon and in ten seconds the whole of the sun had gone and five minutes later it was quite dark.

Every night, when on the guns, I looked out for the Pole Star, the only star I know, it kept getting lower and then one night it had gone, that made me realise how far from home I was.

We always seemed to be voyaging on a great circle of sea, never getting nearer to the horizon, how monotonous it was.

Finally we saw land again and sailed into Cape Town. What a wonderful sight with Table Mountain in the background. We remained there for five days and were allowed on shore when not on duty. The hospitality was very good and Radford and I were invited to a private house where we had a very nice meal. One night we went to the pictures.

The stay in cape Town ended and we moved out and formed up again. The convoy was much smaller, it seemed that half of our convoy had not gone to Cape Town but gone on to Durban and we never joined up with them again.

The conditions were very trying, we were approaching the Equator again and the temperature was rising. One day I wandered round the boat and I worked out that the lifeboats could carry about a thousand, the life rafts about the same number, the remaining three thousand odd would be at the mercy of the sea or the sharks which were pretty plentiful at the time.

Washing of clothing was a problem, the soap would not lather in the salt water and then you had the problem of drying. One of the gunners had an idea and he took his washing into the turret and draped it over a gun. Unfortunately the Captain went up on the bridge and spotted it. He exploded and that night it stated in the ship's orders that troops would not hang their washing on the guns.

I was amazed one morning to see that the rest of the

convoy was miles ahead of us and we were trailing on our own. A convoy never stopped if there was trouble with one of the ships, if they did they would just be sitting targets for any lurking submarines. It appeared that our steering gear had gone wrong and we had completed a circle before it could be put right. After a few hours we caught up and resumed our position in the convoy.

The toilet arrangements were very crude, the seats were just holes in planks, about twenty, and when the sea was rough the sea came up through these holes and you found yourself sitting in several inches of water.

We continued to zigzag up the Indian Ocean, recrossed the equator and the day came when we, with one cruiser as escort, headed East and the rest of the convoy continued North, we then knew that we were going to India. The only cheering thing that happened was that the Pole Star had risen above the horizon again. The Southern Cross was magnificent but the Pole Star was, to me, something of home, something I could see from the back garden.

3. Training in India

About the 10th of June we berthed at Bombay and were thankful to be on land again. We had been eight weeks on the voyage and conditions had been bad but we had got through without trouble from the enemy and this is when shipping losses from submarines were at their highest.

The second day in Bombay we were allowed shore leave. Radford and I went together and found our way to the YMCA. It was late afternoon and they told us that it was too early and would not give us even a cup of tea so we went to an Indian restaurant and had a meal. We walked around the city and then went back on board.

The next day the draft was split up, Radford and I kept together and were posted to the 25th Dragoons. We left by train for Poona where we arrived next morning, we changed trains and later in the day arrived at Nira, about 50 miles from Poona.

We were taken by lorry to the campsite about three miles away, it was called Galunche. It was on a plateau about five hundred feet up and extended about two miles, everything was burnt up and the whole area was covered with rocks just on the surface but not embedded in the ground. The regiment was still on the North West Frontier and did not reach us for three weeks but an advance party was there. So we were set to work building roads and erecting tents. We soon discovered that it was not wise to bend down to pick up a rock, you first kicked it over to make sure there was no snake underneath. Snakes were everywhere and sleeping on the ground, to me, was a nightmare. In time we were issued with charpoys, native bedsteads, wooden frames crisscrossed with rope, they were not too bad, at least they kept us off the ground.

The regiment arrived from Peshawar, a station on the North West Frontier, they were eighty percent regulars, mainly ex-cavalry and very few of them had ever been near a tank. When they left the frontier it was decided not to bring their horses and rather than sell them to the natives who they considered would not give them the care and attention they were used to they had them put away. Many were the tales we were told of hardened old regulars who were in tears when they had to take their horses to be put down.

We spent a few more weeks building roads and when the camp was in good shape we were posted to our various squadrons. I was posted to C squadron and parted from Radford who went to HQ where he went into the RQMS section, made good use of his training as a bank clerk and eventually finished up as the RQMS.

In C squadron we did a lot of drilling and marching, there was nothing else to do as we had no tanks.

We were wearing the tropical kit issued in England, the same as had been issued since the beginning of the century but this was all changed. Shorts which came below the knees were cut to four inches above the knees and our sun helmets, very heavy, at least half an inch thick and made of cardboard were scrapped and were issued with topees, sometimes called pith helmets, they were very light and comfortable. The band round the topee was in regimental colours and in it we carried a safety razor blade. This was to be used in the case of a snake bite, two cuts had to be made diagonally across the bite and as deep as possible to allow the blood to pour out and wash the poison away. I am glad that I never had to make use of this, some of the men did and they survived. Snakes were plentiful and the more deadly were so poisonous that after a bite the victim died within minutes.

We were now divided into Troops and I found myself in No2 Troop and moved into a tent on the edge of the plateau from where we looked across the plains to the Western Ghats about thirty miles away. There were eight of us in the tent and a regular, a corporal, was in charge. He could never make out how it was that we, in his view, old men had been sent to India. When parades were over he always addressed me as Mr Heynes.

I found the birdlife interesting; the house sparrows were the same as at home, larks in the sky, parrots, green with red heads and plenty of vultures. Wherever we established a camp the kite hawks soon found us and always assembled near the cook house. When meals were being served the air was thick with these kites ready to dive and pinch something from your plate as you carried it along to find somewhere to sit down and eat it. When you became experienced you went along bent double with the plate in your left hand, held close to your chest, your right hand carried your mug of tea held just above your left hand. This way you generally reached your destination with the complete meal. Some months later we were out in the wilds and our meal was being served from the back of a lorry. It was a special treat as we were having one real sausage each, I collected mine and went across a bit of open ground to sit under a tree and enjoy my meal. Half way over I moved the plate forward a little so that I could feast my eyes on that wonderful sausage, a kite must have been just over my head because, in a flash, my sausage had gone and I was left with a bleeding thumb where the bird had scratched me. All I had to eat was a thick piece of bread with melted margarine poured over it.

Towards the end of August we received our first mail, it had been posted in April but it was good to be in touch again.

Life was very boring, we finished parades at five o'clock, had our meal at five thirty and after that just sat around until lights out at ten o'clock. The sun went down soon after seven and our only lighting was one hurricane lamp per tent. We had the char wallah, mugs of tea twopence, wads threepence or egg banjos fivepence. These were hard fried eggs between pieces of bread and margarine.

We still had no tanks but each Squadron had about a dozen lorries or trucks and I was the driver of one of the trucks, a Chevrolet 15cwt. It was very old, top speed just under 40mph but it was not safe to drive at that speed because at 36mph you developed front wheel wobble. It was a change from being on fatigues such as spud bashing for whole days at a time.

News came through that we were going to receive our tanks, so the Squadron got down to training, using lorries as tanks we went out on manoeuvres. The squadron Leader used my truck for his tank and I enjoyed driving across country, up and down hills and through rivers. We got on well, he was always the Major and I was always the Trooper. When we stopped we got out and had a cigarette but never offered me one so I smoked my own. It was not meanness on his part, he was a regular officer and I was only a trooper, but things changed later.

We now moved to Dhond, about thirty miles away. What

a change; brick barracks and taps with running water. On top of a hill about half a mile away was a native-run canteen and a cinema. I often went to the cinema with a fellow named Graham, he was a bank clerk and came from Scotland, he was so broad Scotch that I had great difficulty in understanding him. Poor fellow, he got killed later.

Our long-awaited tanks arrived, they were Valentines, about thirty tonnes with a two pounder gun and a machine gun. Troops were now rearranged and training started. I found myself left with a lorry, a Ford three tonnes. I was disappointed but just had to put up with it, at my age, 39, I was considered too old for tank crew.

Training went on well and we were told that the tanks were being taken South about a hundred miles to do some jungle training and I was one of the four drivers whose lorries were going along.

We moved off early one morning and in the afternoon reached our destination. It was right in the middle of an area of jungle, very wild and I liked it. The bird life was wonderful and at nighttime the hyenas and jackals kicked up a terrible din. Being on guard on the outskirts of the camp at night was quite frightening.

The day after we arrived I was detailed to take a corporal and three men to look for bamboo and cut down poles so that racks could be built for ablutions etc. We travelled for a few miles and found some bamboo which we started to hack down. It was growing in clumps, some of the canes were 6 inches thick and very tall, most of the canes carried three inch thorns. By the time my lorry was loaded our denims were badly torn and when we returned to camp the MO put iodine on all our scratches.

Another day I went off with an officer and six men, we

drove along a jungle track and after about ten miles stopped, the officer and men got out. They were to climb a hill on the left of the track and would go down on the other side. I was ordered to drive on for about three miles when I would reach a river, I was to cross it and a short distance along the track I would come to a village where I was to wait for them. I drove off and reached the river and carried on across it. It was only about two feet deep and then I continued along the track but no village appeared. I carried on, the track was rising and getting narrower. After a few more miles I found myself driving with steep rocks on my right and a sheer drop on the left. I decided I was getting nowhere so drove on until I reached a spot where I considered the track was wide enough for me to turn. In driving tests they have three point turns but this must have taken me nearer to twenty three points to turn. I drive back to the river, stopped and had a bathe.

Two hours later the Officer and men arrived, I told him that I had not seen the village and he said that it was there but out of sight from the track.

Life was very pleasant in this bit of jungle, and not being tank crew I had plenty of time to walk around and observe the bird life.

One day I was on duty with my lorry and had to report to the cookhouse, there we filled up with huge chunks of meat, which had gone bad, it seemed that half the fresh meat we received was uneatable. We drove away and reached a clearing where waiting for us were a lot of vultures. They hardly moved away as we threw the meat out, it was like feeding a flock of turkeys.

After three weeks the jungle training ended but instead of returning to Dhond we drove South West, making for the coast where we were to remain for a week for a rest. On the way we drove for at least thirty miles through nothing but bamboo, it was getting on towards a hundred feet tall and as it grew at the rate of ten inches a day the noise made by the replacement of branches was almost deafening. We reached the coast at a place named Karwar and there we camped in a wood of fir trees which stretched down to the beach. We slept on the ground which was sand and I have always found it one of the hardest things to sleep on. After making our beds, a ground sheet and one blanket, we erected our mosquito nets. This we did in the early evening and one fellow, when he went to get into bed later on found a snake inside.

Most of the day was spent bathing, the sun was so hot that in addition to our PT shorts we wore our pith helmets. Watching the natives with nets was very interesting but it was disconcerting to see that as well as fish they caught a number of snakes.

After this pleasant break we returned to camp and the news which greeted us was that our Valentine tanks were being taken away to be replaced with Stuarts, light American tanks about 15 tons. This did not affect me but it did mean a lot of fresh training for the tank crews.

One afternoon I was returning from a journey and as I neared the camp I pulled up to watch a crow which was pecking away at the remains of a carcass, it was not far away and as I watched a vulture landed and took over. The crow fluttered a few feet and must have been in a terrible rage by the noise it was making. It kept looking in my direction and I was amazed to see it dash forward and seize some of the tail feathers of the vulture and start pulling with all its might. It had no effect as the vulture was at least ten times as heavy as the crow. As I started up they both flew away but I will always remember this little incident.

Some months after this I was driving the Squadron Leader for him to spy out the countryside where the next day they were going to have some tank manoeuvres. We were driving up a hillside, there was no road and I was picking my way between the rocks that were lying around until we reached a point where the rocks were too close together for me to drive between. We both jumped out and pushed the rocks aside that were in the way, they were not embedded just lying the surface. When we got back in the lorry the Squadron Leader said "you are not as old as I thought you were (I was 39) how would you like to be on the next course we have and if all is well be a gunner in my tank?" I thanked him and said that I would like to do.

Some weeks later a course started and I was on it. Having done all this before at Bovington and Lulworth to me it was like a refresher course and I quite enjoyed it. The Stuarts were very easy to handle and very nippy. One day we were out with our instructor and he was sending us out in turn, the trip was over the plain, in and out between a lot of rocks and then a straight run home over fairly smooth ground. When my turn came I put my foot down on the run home and got up past 40mph. I expected a ticking off but all the sergeant said was "Pop, you seemed to be enjoying yourself". One thing we did not like about these tanks was that, for the driver to get in, the turret had to be turned with the gun at right angles to the front of the tank and then a hole in the floor of the turret coincided with an opening in the top of the driver's compartment. You squeezed your way in and then the turret was turned by the person in the turret, the driver had no means of doing this. As we were running on high octane spirit and the temperature was in the hundreds there was always, on the back of one's mind - *what happens if she catches fire.*

Another day we were out driving, the sergeant was sitting on the outside of the tank, near the front, I was in the turret waiting for my turn to drive and driving was a trooper who never did anything right. We were driving across some paddy fields, there were no hedges instead there were ridges of earth, in places up to eight feet high and it was good practice to drive over these. The thing to do was to stop at the bottom, get into lowest gear, let the clutch in gently and put your foot down but ease up just before you reached the top, brake and hold the tank at the top of the ridge, then let it balance over. The poor driver did everything wrong, he charged at the ridge, lost his nerve and put his foot on the clutch and we slid back down. After at least half a dozen tries he put his foot down and kept it there and we went over the top and down the other side, gathering speed and there, just in front of us, was a big open well. The driver pulled hard on his right stick and braked and we finished just alongside the edge of the well. I think I died a thousand deaths during those few seconds.

The course finished and I passed and was now a fully qualified gunner mechanic which meant that I was primarily a gunner but able to take over the driving and maintenance of the tank if required. This entitled me to an increase of 6d per day in my pay.

Training went on and became very boring, sometimes we would go a full week without taking the tank out, standing around pretending to do maintenance where there was none to be done.

The day came when I was told to report to the Squadron Office, I did so and the Squadron Leader was waiting for me. He told me that the Squadron Clerk was leaving to go for a commission and he would like me to take over. He promised me that when the tank went out for training I would be with it and when we went to war I would be his gunner.

I took the job, it was easy and kept me off parades.

After a few weeks our tanks were taken from us and we were told that we were going to move to Ranchi, this was the other side of India and a jumping off place for Burma. I was given the job of driving the Unit Repair Lorry and had two fitters with me and we took it in turn to drive. It was a seventeen-hundred-mile journey, most of it over dirt roads with dust inches deep. The system was to travel for two days and then one day for maintenance.

We went as far North as Lucknow and had two nights there, the second day being for maintenance. We slept in the old barrack building where our troops made a final stand in the Indian Mutiny. The walls were six feet thick and overhead were punkahs which helped to keep the place cool, not operated by punkah wallahs as in the past but by electric motors. Outside, in the open, the temperature was 120 in the shade, so it was pretty hot working on our lorries.

We now headed South and arrived at the Ganges where one night we bathed from the steps of a native temple, the natives did not look too pleased as this was considered, by them, a very sacred area. Eventually we reached Benares the sacred city where white man was not allowed so we camped on the outskirts. From here we crossed over the river by driving along a railway bridge, it was just under 2 miles wide and there was just room at the side of the rails for our lorries with less than a foot to spare. As we were only allowed to use the bridge as a special concession we had to fit in between train times and had to get a move on.

From Benares we continued our journey and two days later reached Ranchi.

It was a poor camp, no brick buildings, just bamboo huts known as bashas, the roofs were made with layers of palm leaves and, some were infested with rats and some had snakes in them and there were bugs in all of them.

We had our new tanks, more American ones called Lees, 35 tonnes 350hp engines. They were pretty roomy, downstairs, the driver, wireless operator, 75mm gunner and his loader and in the turret, the tank commander, 37mm gunner and his loader. We went through all the training again and then we were ready to move when required. The monsoon season was with us so we were kept bogged down most of the time. I was still Squadron Clerk as well as gunner so I had plenty to do as we were receiving a number of intakes to bring us up to war strength. At night I slept in the Squadron Office, just another basha, with open spaces in the walls for windows. One night I was lying on my charpoy waiting to go to sleep, it was after lights out. I heard padded footsteps approaching and as they got nearer there was very heavy breathing. The animal was just outside the hut and I felt petrified, every second expecting to see a dark form in one of the window spaces. The animal padded on round and then I heard a dog barking wildly as it chased towards my hut. When it was quite near it started yelping madly and went off into the distance. The padded footsteps also went off into the distance and I breathed again. I shall never know what animal it was, it was heavy and had pads. Was it a tiger? We were in tiger country.

One day the Squadron Leader was doing a lot of paperwork and after a while he called me over. He had a list which showed the number of men we had in each trade in one column and in the second one the numbers required to bring us up to war strength and the third column was headed deficiency. He had filled in the first two columns and in the third, deficiency one, had repeated the number of men we already had. I glanced at it and said that I thought he had made a mistake in the third column as deficiency was what we required and not what we already had, Sir. He did not say a word but seized the list and made off towards the Orderly Room.

Half an hour later he returned but as the Sergeant Major was in the office he said nothing but waited until he went out and then he said "Heynes, you were right". I just nodded.

The months passed by, reinforcements arrived and all the crews were made up to war strength. Then rumours started to fly around and one day I found myself typing up lists of all our tank crews as submitted by Troop Leaders giving details of their trades and ages. These lists were taken to the Orderly Room by the Officers where they had to be vetted. I did not feel too happy when I noticed that at 39 I was at least 5 years older than the odd one or two who were over 30 and some even under twenty. Later in the afternoon one of our Officers came back from the Orderly Room and said that he did not think that I would be in the crews. He thought that this news would cheer me up but I told him that it did not and that I hoped Major Horn would get me in. An hour afterwards the Squadron Leader came in and said "Heynes, you are going to be my gunner". I thanked him.

4. Burma

The next day we were told that we were moving on the following morning, so I spent a lot of time burning all our papers except for lists of the men, their qualifications and addresses of next of kin. the last night we had an issue of beer, two bottles per man, as some did not drink the supply was ample. If a tiger had come into my hut that night, I would not have noticed it.

Next day we moved off in our tanks and after a few miles we waited for some tank transporters to pick us up. They took us about 30 miles to a railway siding where we waited a week for a train with special rolling stock to take us to Calcutta.

In this place there was no canteen and we had no newspapers so every morning either Wilkinson or myself were allowed in the officers' tent where we listened to the radio news and made notes. From these we wrote out something which we could hang on the men's notice board. One morning when I was listening the newsreader mentioned that the war had just completed its fifth year. I put this down in my news and added that one war lasted a hundred years.

We got our tanks on the rolling stock, very old and looking most unsafe, then covered them with tarpaulins for disguise. I rode on one of these sideless trucks, there was a man on each, the reason being to put out any fire which started from the sparks the old engine spouted out whenever we came to an incline. Eventually we reached

Calcutta and finished up at the docks where we unloaded
and drove the tanks under cover. Strict security
precautions were taken, our berets were taken from us and
we were issued with side caps as in those days only tank
men used black berets and, no doubt, the Japs had their
spies about. We spent a month in Calcutta waterproofing
our tanks so that they could be taken in tank landing craft
to the shores of Burma and land in anything up to six feet
of water. American tank landing craft arrived at the docks
and we loaded up. We moved off early one morning,
down the Hoogly to the Bay of Bengal. Some two hours
after our start we saw about a dozen bombers, flying in the
direction of Calcutta, these we thought were Japs, and later
it was confirmed. They plastered the docks area, so we
were lucky.

I found the journey down the Hoogly very interesting as
not long before I had read a book by a big game hunter
who had made this trip. He told how, from his boat, he
had seen a tiger sunbathing on one of the many islands in
the river and, although he had his rifle with him, he could
not bring himself to fire at it as it was such a magnificent
animal.

The landing craft, being American, was well fitted out, we
had beds with spring mattresses and in the wall of the
canteen was a tap from where we helped ourselves to hot
coffee, a sugar basin was near and we could have as much
as we liked. The Americans fed us on this trip, chicken,
vegetables, tinned fruit and ice cream. What a change
from the meals we had been having.

We continued through the night and next day until late
evening when the coast of Burma appeared. It was a full
moon, a cloudless sky and from where we anchored, about
400 yards out, we had a good view of the jungle stretching
away into the distance. There seemed to be a purple haze

over everything.

The front of the craft was opened up and the slipway let down, the first tank moved forward and into the sea and then slowly made its way to the shore. We followed in turn, it was a strange journey, with the waves well up to the turret but all went well. Overhead were 2 of our bombers to hide the noise made by the tank engines. When we reached the shore we turned right and drove along for about 3 miles keeping to the edge of the sea so that the tide, which was coming in, would obliterate our tracks.

We reached a point where the jungle came very near to the sea and there we drove up a narrow track into thick jungle and continued along for about three miles and there we found our advance party waiting for us. The tanks were dispersed and driven under trees so that they were not visible from the air. The undergrowth was thick and as we cut it away round the tank to make room for us to sleep two snakes squirmed their way into thicker growth nearby.

The place we landed was called Elephant point, some ten miles south of Cox's Bazaar.

Being tired out we laid out our ground sheets and wrapped in our one blanket with our haversacks as pillows went to sleep. The next day we got organised and erected a tarpaulin overhead stretching from the side of the tank and over the place where we slept. Next we cut a way through the vegetation to the place where food was served out. Our lorries were not with us as there was no road they could use and were about a mile away alongside a usable track. As it was necessary at times for someone to go from the one area to the other it meant walking through this mile of jungle. In the area was a herd of wild elephants with several young ones and a number of times they were seen between the two camps but I was never lucky enough, although many times I heard them trumpeting.

Living in the jungle where the sun did not penetrate had a depressing effect on men who had been used to working in such bright sunshine, so the Medical Officer arranged for the men to spend one day and night on the beach every week. This meant walking the 3 miles down to the beach, carrying blankets, ground sheets and rations but it was well worth the trouble. The stretch we used was lovely silver sand but as we approached it was bright red. This is because it was covered with little red crabs which ran into holes as we got nearer. Most of the time we spent bathing, naked of course, we had no bathing trunks. The food was generally corned beef, dehydrated potatoes and army biscuits with margarine poured on with a spoon. We had no green vegetables so were issued with special pills containing vitamin C, they tasted horrible.

Christmas arrived and we had special rations including Christmas puddings and an issue of beer, warm beer does not taste very good. In the afternoon I went fishing in the river about two miles away, my companion was another bank clerk, Jim Alcock. We caught some little fish which inflated themselves when landed, they looked like tennis balls with mouths and tails. They floated on top of the water when thrown back but after a minute or two returned to their normal size then swam away. We also came across some mud fish which spent a lot of time climbing trees.

It was decided that as the guns had not been fired for more than two months we needed some practice. The first thing to do was to test and adjust the sights. This was the job of the gunner so I got to work on the 37mm which was my gun, up in the turret. This fired a shell which dropped 4 feet at 600 yards so I had to pick an object 600 yards away, remove the firing pin from the breech end of the barrel and with some grease stick two pieces of cotton across the muzzle end forming a cross. Looking through the hole where the firing pin had been removed the spot where the cotton crossed was noted. Moving to your periscope you adjusted so that the spot where the horizontal line and the vertical line crossed was four feet below the spot your barrel pointed to. Great care had to be taken as everything depended on your accuracy. With these guns it was possible to be dead accurate and if three men were standing side by side at 600 yards and you aimed at the middle one you would hit one of them with nearly every shot.

We did our practice shoot and then cleaned the guns, as our supply of rags had gone astray I decided to tear up my sheets, a present from the Indian Government to every British soldier when he arrived in India. These sheets were rather grubby and from now on we would not be getting undressed at night so they would not be needed, and the gun had to be in good condition as the next time it fired would be at the Japs.

There were a number of hornbills about and it was a strange sight to see them flying overhead with their enormous beaks stretching so far in front of their bodies, you wondered how they were able to keep up.

A few days later we had a visit from Lord Louis Mountbatten, he made a speech to the regiment and I remember him saying "It is easy for me to tell you what to do because when you are doing it I will be sitting on my ass in Delhi". He was well thought of by the forces.

Soon after we moved out at night and early in the morning took our tanks on board some barges which transported us up river and we landed within a few miles of an area where fighting was taking place.

We moved off after dark and finished up in a valley called Chumbra with the jungle clad Mayu Range towering above us. We dispersed and put camouflage netting over the tanks. We were warned to show no lights after dark and as far as possible to keep out of sight in the daytime.

At night we could hear the rattle of machine and rifle fire and in the daytime our dive bombers passed overhead, returning in a few minutes after they had shed their loads.

A few nights later we moved again but this was only a short journey and we pulled into some jungle where we laid up the next day. Night came and we moved out and continued until we reached the bank of a tidal river where we had to wait for the tide to recede sufficiently for us to cross, and having done this we found shelter and had breakfast.

The Japs had some positions a short distance away known as Razabil Fortress, a ridge, between one and two hundred feet high. They had dug themselves in with tunnels joining up both sides of the ridge, we had made many attacks and suffered many casualties, so a new kind of attack was to be made. Dive bombers were to come in followed by heavy bombers which would drop 2,000 pounders in the dust created by the bombs dropped by the dive bombers. We would then move in and shell and machine gun the fortress area and the infantry would move forward and complete the job.

The time for the attack was 12 o'clock, so just before that time we started moving forward so that at 5 past 12 we would be in a position in the open facing the fortress. On the dot the dive bombers came over and dropped their bombs on target. Clouds of dust arose as the heavy bombers appeared and released their bombs. This was all according to plan but unfortunately one bomb aimer mistook the dust stirred up by the tanks for the dust caused by the dive bombers and we had three 2,000 pounders dropped across our track. There were terrific explosions and our tank rocked like a ship in a gale. The lid on the turret was open and as I looked up the air was black with earth and we heard shrapnel hitting the side of the tank. Three of the tanks were put out of action, some men were killed and some wounded. I did not feel too good, rather angry I think, some clot of a bomb aimer had been careless. After a few minutes we moved forward into the open and there in front of us was Razabil Fortress.

The shells started falling near but no direct hit. Our 75mm guns opened up on positions where the guns were likely to be and before long no more shells were falling so they must have been on target.

As I sat in the turret, with my eyes glued to the periscope, the landscape was spread before me with the ridge in the background about 400 yards away, pitted with bomb craters.

The ground to the ridge was an area of rough land with patches of scrub jungle. Halfway to the ridge there was a line of telegraph poles and on the wires were some bee eaters, very colourful birds, they kept flying up for the flies and returning to the wires, paying no attention to the firing which was going on all around them. After a while the Squadron Leader ordered me to machine the patches of jungle. This was kept up most of the afternoon and then the infantry moved forward but when they got close to the ridge they found that the Japs were still there so had to retreat and the ridge was not captured. We pulled out and returned along the track to the place in the jungle used as HQ and Horn got out and went to give in his report. We were all dying for a cup of tea so two of us jumped out hoping to get a kettle boiled, we soon gave it up as we were in range of some snipers and they were getting too close for comfort.

Horn returned and we moved to an arranged rendezvous about a mile away where we were going to shelter for the night. After dark tanks are very vulnerable especially in jungle country, it would have been so easy for the Japs to infiltrate and throw a few grenades starting fires and panic. The cooks were waiting with a meal prepared, I expect I would turn up my nose at it today but that night it seemed to be perfect and the mug of tea was wonderful. I was not on guard so had a good night's sleep. Next morning we were up before daybreak, had breakfast, waited about for the order to move when a number of Jap fighters appeared and started machine gunning and bombing a position about half a mile away. Thank heavens they did not spot us; we would have been sitting targets.

After they had gone we moved back to positions near where we had been the day before, doing a lot of shelling and machine gunning never seeing the enemy but using up a lot of ammunition. Late in the afternoon my machine gun was so hot that even after I had taken my finger off the button it continued to fire odd rounds. We pulled out to make for night shelter and as my gun was still firing odd rounds every two or three minutes I raised the elevation so that none of the other tanks would get hit. As we moved along we could see a cloud of dark smoke ahead and when we reached it found out it was my old Unit Repair lorry. The chaps said that a bullet came out of the blue, went into the petrol tank and it went up in flames. No-one was hurt and they were able to save their personal kit. I looked back along the track we had come and I felt convinced that my gun fired that bullet but I dare not tell them so.

It may have been that night or another soon after when it was my turn to be on guard. We had pulled out and reached the spot where we were parking for the night, it was overlooked by a hill half a mile away which at that time was occupied by the Japs. There were odd patches of jungle and the tanks were tucked away in these but behind them away from the hill was a paddy field. We had five on guard at a time, two pairs manning machine guns facing both ways along the track and I was the odd man out. I expected to be left to walk around the tank area but no, the guard commander wanted me to patrol around the paddy field which had thick jungle along the far side. He went round with me the first time, we crossed the paddy and along the edge of the jungle for about a quarter of a mile and then tuned back to the tank area. Next time I went round on my own and by now it was quite dark and I was listening to the sounds coming from the jungle, hoping they were made by animals. In places the vegetation was up to my middle and there were odd trees about. I hoped that I would not step on a snake. My system was to go slowly when near the tanks but speeding up as I went from them. How thankful I was when my two hours were over and my relief took over. Four hours later I was on again and by this time the moon was shining brightly overhead. The wind started blowing and shadows were moving and to me it was much worse than in the dark. I felt convinced that there were Japs crawling around and I clutched my tommy gun under my arm and must have been very near to panicking. I never felt so lonely in all my life. My spell ended and I lay down on my ground sheet alongside the tank. How lovely to be back home, the tank was the only home I had then.

After a few days we were pulled out and returned to Chumbra, the tanks were badly in need of a service and we all needed a rest.

After a week or so we were visited by a General and he told us that the next evening we were going to cross the Mayu Range by means of the Ngakyedauk Pass, rest the following day and the day after that take a company of Ghurkas on our tanks, go through Jap held country and capture their HQ some six miles away. We were told to hold this position until relieved. We did not like the idea at all. To begin with nothing bigger than a 3 ton lorry had been over the pass before and if we did capture the Jap HQ holding it was going to be quite a problem.

However, next evening, after dark, we started off and reached the foot of the pass. The road from there was very steep in places and not very wide. It was somewhere near the highest point we reached a hairpin with a sheer drop of 200 feet on the one side and rocks on the other, we had to reverse a number of times and in the darkness, it was most hair-raising. We met natives going in the opposite direction, a few at first and then hosts of them. It seemed strange to us that they were moving about in the middle of the night, we did not know that the Japs were pushing down from the North and the villagers were fleeing from them.

As we neared the end of the pass we came to a section where the road zigzagged 7 or 8 times and the hairpins at the end of each straight bit were so sharp and steep that orders were given to switch on headlights. What a sight to see tanks going in one direction and a few feet below some going the other way and so on down. We reached the end of the pass as it began to get light and parked under trees to be out of sight from the air. We rested that day but had several alerts when zeros visited the area fortunately doing no harm. They were very good fighters, very like our spitfires, a little slower but more manoeuvrable. As well as machine guns they could carry one 100 pound bomb which was carried in the cockpit and rolled overboard by the pilot.

Night came and as far as I was concerned I was not looking forward to next morning. During the night we had several alerts and news reached us that the Japs were approaching. On one of the alerts a corporal took three of us up the ridge, after 30 yards he told one to remain there, 30 yards further up he left another man behind and he and I continued a bit higher where he left me and he returned down to the tank. The jungle ahead was quite thick but where I was was fairly clear so I stood near a bush so as not to be too conspicuous.

After a while I heard a noise in the jungle and it was men moving about and talking. Fortunately no one appeared so when the corporal fetched me some time later I told him and he and I agreed that it was probably some natives moving away from the Japs. Next morning we knew that it was the Japs and that they were making for the foot of the pass.

5. The Battle of the Admin Box

Half an hour before daybreak we were up and in our tanks for an hour, this pattern back to the days of cavalry when attacks were always made at daybreak or at sunset. When allowed to dismount we started the Primus stove to make some tea and have breakfast. Then the order came to move without delay, the Japs had captured the pass and were getting near.

The Primus and lots of things were left behind as we pulled out, we were not going through to capture the Jap divisional HQ, they had captured ours. We moved along the track towards our HQ and as we went we met lots of Indian troops fleeing towards the pass, they did not know the Japs were there before them, in fact we were completely surrounded. We reached our old HQ which was now a smouldering ruin. Our troops were coming in from outlying areas, looking very dejected. We did some shelling and machine gunning into the jungle where the Japs were. Rain started to come down, so we turned round and returned along the track to a position about a mile from the foot of the pass. We had difficulty on the way, our tank tracks were rubber covered and we were unable to get a grip on the wet surface and when we came to an incline we stopped dead. This meant getting out and putting things called grousers on the tracks, about three feet apart. They were metal claws which stuck out about three inches and this gave us some grip and enabled us to move again. We reached our destination with a stream on one side of the track and paddy fields on the other. The Squadron Leader jumped out and said he was going to a conference and would be back in half an hour. It had stopped raining, so I jumped out and taking soap and a towel went down to the stream, waded across to some shingle on the far side, undressed and got in to have a bath. An infantryman came out of the jungle nearby and told me to get into the side as the Japs were just above us and would be able to see me where I was. I did so, finished my wash down, dressed and nipped back across the stream and into the tank, feeling much fresher.

Whilst I was away some of the chaps had been looking around and found half a crate of condensed milk and a blow lamp. We did all our cooking with that blow lamp from then on. We made a pot of tea and with some army biscuits and corned beef had our first meal of the day. Snipers were near so we had to move behind the tank for shelter.

The squadron Leader returned from the conference and it was decided that before dark the tanks would form up in the middle of the paddy fields, facing outward, like in the days of the old covered wagons and red Indians.

The paddy area was just over a mile long and perhaps three quarters of a mile wide with one or two patches of jungle in places. A temporary divisional HQ was set up and the area was known as "Admin Box" or the Box. Just before the sun went down we formed up in a triangle with most of the tanks on the two sides away from the track and on the other side where the stream was some 10 feet below the level of the track trenches were dug on the bank of the stream and these were manned by HQ staff, cooks, lorry drivers and batmen. Japs occupied the tops of all the ridges and hills so we were looked down on from all sides.

The sun would soon be going down so we were given an issue of rum, to keep us warm we were told but I think it was to give us courage … we needed it. We found ourselves in a position which in all our training we had been told to avoid. Tanks were so vulnerable after dark unless they had a line of defence between them and the enemy. Without that line of defence the enemy could so easily creep up and throw a few hand grenades and one landing in the turret would be enough to put the tank and crew out of action.

I was just about to take my place in the tank when some tanks on my right started firing, others joined in so I fired a few rounds with my machine gun into the jungle about 150 yards away. After a few minutes I decided there was nothing to fire at so I stopped and stood up and the sight of all these tanks belching out sheets of flame and the streams of tracers pouring into the jungle opposite was awe inspiring from our side, what the Japs thought when they saw it from their side I do not know but later on we decided it made them hesitate from making a frontal attack in the darkness that night. We just sat in our positions in the tank and waited, an hour later the moon came up, a full moon, and shone through the rest of the night. It had seemed a very long night and we were very thankful when it ended and we dispersed our tanks, to have remained in the triangle in daylight would have left us easy targets for the enemy gunners and bombers.

We moved to one of the odd patches of jungle and had breakfast. Near us was a battery of medium guns, two of them, they were 5-inch calibre and fired shells of about a hundred weight and they spent most of the day firing on open sights at likely Jap positions in the jungle opposite. As some of the shells were exploding less than 400 yards away the shrapnel was coming back to us, so we had to take cover on the lee side of the tank. When it was noticed that the Japs were concentrating on any spot we were called to action and did our usual shelling and machine gunning to relieve the pressure. At times we were required to leave the Box and go along tracks to get round behind the Jap positions and shell them from there. Occasionally the journey was several miles and being on our own we prayed that the tank would not break down. Later the Japs started laying land mines in places and we lost some tanks.

The second night was the same as the first, the moon came up later and this gave one more hour of darkness when we were most vulnerable. My gun loader was never a very clean chap, when we settled in the tank for the night, he used to remove his boots and the smell coming from his feet was terrible, his socks could not have been washed for weeks.

During the evening we were told that a wireless message had been received from HQ at Delhi saying that relief was on the way and would reach us in 24 hours. Actually an infantry regiment was making its way over another pass 6 miles to the North and it took them 3 weeks to reach us. the next day a message was received from Churchill "hold on, you are making history, I am watching the battle with interest".

This was the first time that the Jap advance had been halted, they could not get their transport through as we were in the way but we were only in the way because we could not get out of it.

The Japs had no heavy guns in the immediate area but there was one big one about 4 miles away and with this they used to shell us for about 10 minutes every morning and again in the evening. You heard a bang in the distance then for the next 15 seconds nothing, then something like an express train approaching at terrific speed, over the last few hundred yards the sound was deafening, then the explosion. If you were outside you got up from the ground where you had been lying with your head buried in your arms and looked round to see if anybody had caught it.

One morning one of these shells landed some twenty yards from the tank but fortunately we all happened to be inside. However the shrapnel did penetrate a steel locker on the back of the tank in which, among other things, we kept our plates and mugs and we found ourselves with only 3 mugs and 4 plates between the seven of us. After that Major Horn who lost both plate and mug shared with me but always insisted that I used them first. The belief was that the Japs kept this gun in a tunnel which we knew about, and trotted it out for short spells and then back again. Our 5-inch guns spent the greater part of one day firing at the position but it had no effect, the shells continued to come over as before and it was decided that the maps we had were not accurate.

Our dive bombers were very busy, they came over in formations of twelve, 4 rows of 3 and dived down on the positions held by Japs at the top of the pass. We saw bombs leave the planes at the last possible moment and as they pulled out of their dives just missing the treetops the bombs exploded.

We had a visit from a Zero, at the time we were sitting in the tank, waiting for the Squadron Leader to return from a conference. The plane dived low and just passed over us and as I looked up through the turret I saw a bomb roll over the side of the cockpit. It wiped out the crew of one of the medium guns and put the gun out of action. Horn was very restless and that afternoon we moved away from the paddy area to a place where the ground sloped up from us to a hill in the background. The ground ahead was not thick jungle, so it was possible to see if anyone was moving about. Horn was looking through his field glasses and then he said "Heynes, I can see some Japs". He indicated where they were by the clock face system. I looked where he indicated and saw some men moving about under a tree. He ordered me to fire high explosive shells when I was ready and continue until he told me to stop. I fired nine rounds as quickly as my loader could reload and then he ordered me to stop. He said "Heynes, you killed a lot of Japs then". I felt pleased, at last I knew that some of my shooting had had an effect. I felt no sorrow, this was war.

We returned to the paddy fields and got ready for the night. It was decided that two only need remain awake at a time and the others could sleep but in their positions. I asked Horn if, when I was not on guard, I could lie down on the back of the tank, he said that I could. I was so relieved to get away from the smell of those feet. To get comfortable, lying on top of shovels, pickaxes, chains and other gear and the kit bags, was difficult but eventually I did and dozed off. Before long, however, the remaining medium gun started firing and every time it did the blast lifted me up, perhaps only an inch or so but after that finished I did manage to get a bit of sleep before the time came for me to go on guard. Another night had gone by without an attack by the Japs.

The snipers were quiet at night but you could hear clashes between patrols and occasionally the Jap machine guns would open up. They sounded very slow and deep like ha ha ha and we referred to them as laughing guns. Fires appeared on the ridges at night and we understood that the Japs were burning their dead.

We were often visited by two of our fighters, Hurricanes, and they were known to us as the Twins. They did a bit of firing at Jap positions and then cleared off and quite often, soon after they had gone, Zeros came on the scene. One morning some twenty Zeros were seen approaching at about 7,000 feet and from the other direction we saw a number of Spitfires at about the same height. We expected them to meet overhead and to have a grandstand view of a dog fight but the Japs had cold feet and turned tail with the Spitfires in pursuit. We never heard what happened.

Our supplies were getting low, food fuel and ammo and we all felt worried so, one day, it was a cheering sight to see two Dakotas overhead they circled round and started dropping supplies. What a lovely sight, blue sky, green jungle, and red, blue, yellow and white parachutes floating down. They visited us daily and, no doubt, this enabled us to hold out. They generally dropped from 300 feet but one day there was a strong wind and we watched the bulk of the drop drift into Jap held territory. Sometimes the parachutes failed to open so we had to keep our eyes open when the Dakotas were about. Sugar was packed loosely into canvas sacks, about 2 feet square. Looking rather like a cushion and these were pushed overboard and always landed flat. One day we were doing odd jobs on the tank when a drop was on, the 75mm gunner had raised the lid over his gun and was standing in the opening which was about 2 feet 6 inches square. He dropped something onto the ground so jumped down to pick it up and as he did so one of these sugar bags fell into the tank. Had he not jumped down his neck would have been broken. The bag burst and there was sugar everywhere, we gathered it up and after that had lovely sweet tea.

The fourth night arrived and the driver and I had permission to spend the period, when not on guard, on our groundsheets under the tank. Not very nice really, the ground was all uneven and we only had about three inches clearance above our bodies. The moon was rising much later now so we had several hours of darkness. I do not think I had been to sleep when firing started. We both crawled out and up the front of the tank and into the turret. Most of the tanks in the immediate area were firing so I got my machine gun going and sprayed the area in front. Horn now appeared, I think he had been lying down behind the tank, and took charge. He got us firing high explosives. It seemed that there were some Indian troops in trenches near the edge of the jungle in front of us and we could hear them shouting. Eventually we ceased firing and waited till morning. When it got light, we counted fourteen dead Japs in the area in front of us, the nearest about twenty yards away and over by the edge of the jungle were some Indian dead. Some Indian troops were sent out to gather up the bodies and later they used a bulldozer to make a grave and buried them. I noticed that the Indians carried their own dead but dragged the Japs.

Later in the morning I went into the bit of jungle in front of the tanks for toilet purposes and wandered round a bit. I came across a trench and inside was a blood-soaked blanket and a Jap steel helmet. I thought I would take the helmet as a souvenir, stooped down and picked it up but inside was half a man's head so I threw it down, feeling pretty sick.

More excursions during the day, did a lot of firing but saw no Japs. Late in the afternoon we were back in the paddy fields, doing a bit of maintenance on the tank and guns and not far from an ammunition dump the Jap bombers had hit the day before and it was still burning with odd shells bursting and shrapnel flying about. We were in this position because it was sheltered from snipers and the risk from the shrapnel was less than that from the snipers. We had finished our jobs so the driver and I moved a little distance from the tank to have a smoke. We were talking when we heard a whir of shrapnel and he fell down. He was badly shaken and there was a deep gash on his shoulder where the shrapnel had hit him. It was quite a big piece, about 10 inches by 2 and when I picked it up it was too hot to hold. Some first aid men took him to the hospital, just another basha, where he was treated and they wanted him to stay in but he got out of it and spent the night with the Unit Repair Outfit chaps who lived in a spare tank, doing a bit of firing when they felt like it. They could always say they thought they saw some Japs. During the night the Japs entered the hospital, killed all the wounded and the three Medical Officers. It was in no man's land between positions held by us and by them. They had no finer feelings, after they captured the pass they let one convoy of wounded men go through but when another one started they killed all the men and overturned the red cross vans.

During the day barbed wire entanglements had been erected round the area where the tanks parked at night with an opening for us to enter which was closed up before sundown so we felt a bit more secure. We dug trenches between the tanks and some of us spent the night in these, during the period when not on guard we found that we could sleep by leaning over the parapet. Plenty of fires on the ridge opposite, Verey lights were going off but nothing happened to worry us. Morning came and after a night with some sleep I was feeling pretty good. I had a wash and a shave, only one mug of water for the two, one of the young boys said "Pop, you look well" and asked me how old I was. I remember saying that I would be 40 in a week's time and that I was thinking of having breakfast in bed on my birthday.

During the morning a Major from the West Kent Regiment came alongside the tank and asked Horn if he would help him. It appeared that his regiment was fighting in the hills a few miles away and from time to time they had to send runners with despatches for HQ. The previous day two of them had been killed and that morning another one, all at the same spot, by a sniper. Horn was only too willing to help so we moved off along a track with the infantry Major kneeling behind the turret and directing us. We moved slowly off the track through some thick undergrowth. The Major spotted the sniper and pointed him out to us. He was near the top of a tree about 80 yards away and I could see him quite clearly through the branches. Horn told me to fire when ready. One short burst was enough and his body crashed to the ground. I felt rather like a butcher but perhaps today there are one or two living in West Kent or some part of England who would not be if the sniper had not been put away.

The Jap pressure on one of the ridges was mounting so it was decided to do something about it. The spot was where the stream flowed alongside the foot of the ridge, with, on the other side, the ground sloping up to a track. We had three tanks on the track facing across the stream and some infantry in the jungle at the foot of the ridge over the stream. We were down below the tanks by the side of the stream but Horn was in wireless touch with them and gave the firing orders. An infantry officer was standing by the side of the tank with a walkie talkie, in touch with the infantry.

I was, with 3 other members of our crew, sitting on the ground near the tank, behind us were 4 lorries laden with pontoons and another lorry in which all the drivers were sitting, they were all Indians. The tanks started firing and there was a terrific noise, so much so that we did not hear the engines of two zeros flying overhead. Somebody shouted "Zeros" and I looked up and saw one of them turn and dive towards us. He was machine gunning and bullets were flying all around. Two of the chaps got into the tank, another one dived into a trench and Horn shouted to me to get under the tank. I went under on my tummy, he went under on his back and the infantry officer crouched at the back of the tank. We had just got under when there was a terrific explosion. It seemed as if the whole of my body had been hit, and then, for an instant, which seemed to be much longer, there was complete silence and I thought I was dead. Then sound came back, I suppose it was the air rushing back into the vacuum created by the explosion, and I started to wriggle my way out, thankful to find that I could move. There was smoke and flames all around. I stood up, the lorries were enveloped in flames and I heard the screams of the Indian drivers who were in the middle of them. I peered through the smoke and as I watched the tank started moving forward and I saw that the kit bags and other things on the back were on fire. The tank kept moving on, so I ran after it to warn the crew. It continued up the slope and onto the edge of the paddy field where it pulled up. The flames were much higher now and I knew that just under them was the fuel tank, nearly full, containing some 40 gallons of high-octane spirit.

The tank had stopped in an area where senior officers had dugouts and a number of them were some distance from the tank shouting to the driver to move away. As I reached them the flames shot up higher and the officers dived into the dugouts and I ran between them, jumped up the side of the tank, opened the lid and reached for the fire extinguisher which I played on the flames. Two chaps came out of the turret and gave me a hand and between us we were able to kick the burning kit bags and other things onto the ground. One of the Zeros returned, machine gunning and our Padre, who was in a nearby trench, jumped out and pulled me into shelter. After the Zero had passed over we came above ground and I looked out for the Squadron Leader but he was not there so I said I would go back and look out for him. Our CO, who was standing nearby and said he would take some of them with him and find Major Horn and he ordered a corporal, out of our tank, to take me to a first aid post, which was nearby. I must have looked a very sorry sight, my beret had been blown away in the explosion, my denims were cut by the pieces of shrapnel and I was bleeding quite a lot and feeling shocked. the party which went to look for Horn found him with a shrapnel wound in his throat, the infantry officer was dead, the Indian drivers were dead and the chap who jumped into the trench was badly burned. The Zero had dropped a bomb which landed 10 feet behind the back of the tank.

At the First Aid Post they gave me a cup of tea and a cigarette and phoned for transport to take me to the hospital area. One of our crew came across to see how I was and by now I was feeling very groggy. The places where the shrapnel had gone in were burning and bleeding a lot.

He decided to go back to the tank and fetch my haversack which contained my plate and mug, towel and soap and razor and my cigarettes. I was placed on a stretcher and lifted onto a lorry which took me to the place near the hospital where all the occupants had been killed two days before and was now no longer in use. They took me out of the lorry and placed the stretcher on the ground under a tree. Strewn around me were many more stretchers containing casualties.

An orderly cut my clothes from me, gave me a wash down and plastered me with iodine and put a big piece of cotton wool all round my body, gave me a blanket and put me back on the stretcher.

I slept for some hours and when I woke it was night, a hurricane lamp on the ground a few yards away gave some light and I saw, next to me, on another stretcher, an Indian soldier. The bloody stump of his leg was sticking up and blood was everywhere. Fortunately I was so tired that I went to sleep again and when I woke it was daylight. The Indian soldier had died and had been taken away. I was given a mug of tea and something to eat.

During the day they worked with a bulldozer and with it they dug out a shallow trench alongside the stream which was nearby, and later, the less seriously wounded were carried there on our stretchers where we lay side by side. Next to me was a Captain from HQ, he had managed to escape when the Japs captured their position. We got along together very well and being able to talk with someone helped to pass the time away more quickly. Meals were brought round from an infantry regiment nearby when they had time to do it, you never knew when the next one was coming. One afternoon I was feeling hungry and looking forward to a meal but it did not come till next day. The thing that worried me was that I had no boots or clothes as these had been taken from me when they stripped me down. All I had was a blanket and a steel helmet which was attached to my haversack and I thought what a target I would make if the Japs overrun our position and I attempted to crawl away through the undergrowth. As the sun went down the orderly came round and told us there was to be no more smoking and no talking. As it got dark I used to pull my helmet over my face and wrap the blanket round me. The other side of the stream was thick jungle and often we heard the sound of movement quite near and then rifle fire, being below ground we felt quite safe from the bullets which occasionally whistled by.

On the third day a medical officer came round, the first

visit we had had from one, I told him that I had not yet
had an anti-tetanus injection so he gave me and several of
the others one.

I think it was the same day, in the morning, a patrol of
some 30 infantry men went along the track which passed
by the end of our trench and up the ridge. A little while
later, rifle fire started, they had made contact with the
Japs. Twenty minutes after, they returned, some were
wounded and these they left with us, ten had been left up
the ridge, they would never come down again. I talked
with one of the wounded and he told me that halfway up
the ridge the track divided and the officer had to decide
which way to take. He picked the wrong way and a little
way along they found the Japs waiting for them. No
wonder they were called the PBI, poor bloody infantry. I
told him that I would hate to be in the infantry and he was
just as sure that he would hate to be in a tank. They liked
to see us around when they were in trouble but otherwise
they liked us to keep away, we attracted too much fire. I
liked to think that I was more secure with some armour
plating round me.

When the big gun fired we could hear the shells coming
just the same as out on the paddy fields, I used to pull my
tin hat down over my face and imagine I was safe like the
ostrich does when he buries his face in the sand.

After six days our own Medical Officer came to see me
and he decided to take me back to the tank area where he
had his truck with all the necessary equipment and a trench
where I could make my bed. I walked along to his truck,
barefoot and naked with my blanket wrapped round me
like a sari. When we reached the tank area we stopped at
his trench. I stood by the side of his truck, dropped my
blanket and stood naked in the open. He removed the
cotton wool which had not been looked at since it had

been put round me the day I was wounded. He probed around the wounds and when he felt metal he fished about with some tweezers until he found some shrapnel which he removed. After a while he decided that I had had enough and said that he would have another go next day.

I had a good night's sleep and next morning, my 40th birthday, I did have breakfast in bed, as I had forecast ten days earlier but I did not mean on a stretcher in a trench. To celebrate I had a shave, the first for over a week. I was beginning to feel better and was able to get some odd clothes and walk about.

The Jap pressure was much less now, we understood that they were withdrawing a lot of their troops and taking them up North to the Imphal area where they were making a big push to get into India and down to Calcutta. The snipers were fewer so one day I walked along to the spot where we were bombed. It was soft ground and I soon found our tank tracks and just beyond where they finished where we had backed to be under some cover, was the crater made by the bomb. Nearby was a tangled heap of metal where the lorries had been burnt out, just behind us was a grave with a crude cross made from wood from a packing case and on it was marked "Four Indian other ranks buried here 13th February 1944".

After another week the regiment, which was going to relieve us in 24 hours some three weeks earlier, arrived. Some fighting took place in the pass and the Japs were driven back.

I Felt No Sorrow – This Was War

6. Recovery and Recuperation

The Squadron Leader's batman met me one day and said that the Major was in the hospital area where I had been and that he was going to be evacuated as soon as could be arranged and he said that he would like to see me. We went down together and found the Major, he looked quite comfortable with a charpoy, sheets and blankets and wearing pyjamas. He said he was very pleased to see me and gave me a cigarette. We talked for half an hour and then he said he had been talking to an Officer who was present when our tank pulled up in the HQ area with the kit blazing and he said that my action in jumping on the tank and getting out the fire extinguisher when all the officers were diving for shelter was the bravest he had seen and that he was sorry that, as he was not the senior officer present , he was not qualified to recommend me for a decoration. Horn said that he was sorry that he had not been present as he would have been delighted to do that for me. Later we heard that he had been flown back to England where he had some operations to remove shrapnel from his throat. The chap who dived into a trench when I dived under the tank was also sent home, he was badly burned and his lungs had been affected and my loader, the one with smelly feet, who was in the tank when the shell exploded was sent home with shell shock.

One of the tanks was badly in need of servicing so it was decided to send it back over the pass to a base camp and when it made the journey I was on the back with three others who had been wounded. We passed the Red Cross convoy the Japs had wiped out, a lot of the trucks had been set on fire and most of them had been turned on their sides. There were blood stains all about and the whole thing was a horrible sight. Going over the pass in daytime was bad enough and I was amazed that we had been able to get over at nighttime. We completed the journey over the pass and carried on to the base camp about a mile away.

We reported sick and the MO told me to return in the evening and said "I will examine you when it is quiet". I reported later, it was a bamboo shelter with no sides and rafters going across about 2 feet above my head. I stripped and he told me to put my arms up and hang on to a rafter and then, with a small metal bar he probed into wounds which were still open until he could feel the shrapnel which he removed with tweezers, no local anaesthetic, very crude and painful but effective. I paid several visits and most of my shrapnel had been removed apart from the piece in the left cheek of my bottom and this was very painful when I sat down. As the MO could not find this piece he sent me to the medical centre three miles away and there they cut it out and stitched up the wound. After a fortnight my wounds had all healed up although some shrapnel still remained.

At last I was able to have a good wash all over, so everyday I walked a mile across the plain to a river where I had a good dip.

In our camp was a baby elephant about half a ton, it had been in an area where there was fighting and got separated from the herd and was captured. I visited it every day and gave it bamboo shoots, it loved being played with and I enjoyed my visits. The intention was to train it as a mascot but unfortunately some weeks later it came across some kerosene which a driver was using to clean the engine of his lorry and drank some of it. The poor elephant died the next day.

I was now sufficiently recovered to go on light duties, cleaning guns on reserve tanks most of the time and a few odd jobs.

My turn came to go on guard and with me were my fellow travellers on the back of the tank. One was a corporal and he marched us out to the Guard Post, a trench out in the plain 300 yards from camp. It was a dark night and when I was on duty I noticed a lot of activity out on the plain, Verey lights were being fired and odd rifle shots and I thought it must be some poor infantry unit doing an assault course before being pushed in against the Japs. Next morning we marched back to camp and they told us that they had been up all night, a Jap patrol had gone round the camp and they had been standing to. We, the ones on guard out on the plain had not been warned and had had quite a peaceful night with sound sleep in between our turns on guard.

A few weeks later a notice appeared in Regimental Orders about a Toc H camp at Elephant Point where wounded could go for a week's convalescence. The four of us applied and were allowed the leave. It was very pleasant, we lived in bamboo huts and had one large hut for meals and recreation. The hut where the four of us slept was just along a track leading to a native village, half a mile away. They told us that the previous week a tiger had entered the village at night and carried off a native woman. In spite of that we slept well. We bathed quite a lot and on one day I was playing about in quite a big rocky pool which had been left behind by the tide. It was up to my middle, very clear, and I was watching some fish swimming about when I noticed, just beyond them, a young shark, not big, say three feet long, most unlikely to attack but I was soon out of that pool.

Back to camp and a few weeks later the regiment came back over the pass and joined us. The monsoon season was approaching so the tanks were being pulled out.

We moved about 20 miles and made camp on a hill side and I was back in the Squadron Office but there was not a lot to do. I spent a lot of time watching some weaver birds, it was the nesting season, so they were pretty busy. The nests were built about a foot below a branch, suspended by three strands of tough dry grass and then the framework of the nest was constructed and then they started the weaving, pushing strands from the inside to the outside and then back in and so on until the strand was all used up. I was able to borrow an Officer's field glasses so had a close-up view.

My wounds were beginning to worry me, they were discharging and I was feeling lousy so I reported sick and the MO said that he would arrange for me to go to one of the field hospitals. In the meantime I moved from the Squadron Office, which was a tent, to the ration store, a bamboo affair, which gave me more protection from the weather. The monsoons had now started and as we were in an area where the rainfall was 180 inches in a matter of months the storms were pretty heavy. I slept on the ground in one corner of the store and the rations clerk slept in another, the rations were all stacked in another corner. Next to us, in the other half of the hut, was the sergeants' mess. The top part of the dividing wall was open and there were a lot of rafters stretching the full length of the building. In the afternoon I was lying on my blanket, my eyes just happened to be fixed on a spot at the top of the ration pile when a head appeared. I thought it was just a lizard but it kept getting higher and I realised it was a snake and a pretty big one too. I shouted to the clerk and he went outside, returning with a bamboo pole but when he came back, the snake had moved along the rafters and over the sergeants' mess. He rushed into the mess to warn them, they prodded the snake and it returned to the ration store. One of the sergeants came in and once again prodded the snake and it fell off the rafters and, by good fortune to us, straight into an open tea chest. As it tried to get out and its head appeared over the top the sergeant gave it a mighty wallop and broke its neck. The snake was 8 feet 3 inches long, not a pleasant companion to have in your bedroom.

The next day the MO took me in his Jeep to a field hospital a dozen miles away.

There were a number of bamboo huts , each containing 30 beds with sheets and I was given pyjamas. I was feeling pretty sick, some of the wounds were coming up like boils and I had malaria. They put sticking plaster on the boils and when they were sticking out like hard knobs they tore off the plaster taking with it the core of the wound which generally contained a bit of shrapnel, leaving behind a clean hole which soon healed up. After wearing the pyjamas for a few days, I , like all the others was covered with ring worms so altogether I was feeling very wretched.

We were getting terrific storms, flooding everywhere, quite often you got out of bed into a foot of water. The water for washing was in a tank into which you dipped a bowl, before using it you checked that it contained no leeches, if it did you threw it away and tried again.

After 6 weeks I was moved to Chittagong where the conditions were not so good, we slept on stretchers under a verandah. After 3 weeks I was put on board a hospital ship and we sailed to Madras. At night all lights were on and the decks floodlit to show up the Red Cross, I did not think the Japs would have taken much heed to this so was thankful when we arrived at our destination.

After three weeks at Madras, during which time I had another attack of malaria I was moved to Secunderabad from where I was eventually discharged. The last week in hospital I was on fatigues, spud bashing, the potatoes were very small, had been boiled and we had the wretched job of removing the skins.

7. Preparing for the Next Battle and Returning Home

Discharged with me was another chap from C Squadron, and we went together to a transit camp where we were told that it was up to us to go to the railway station and book up for the journey to our Regiment which, we knew was at Poona. The day was Friday, so we decided to have a quiet weekend and book up on the Monday. This we did and booked the trip for the following day. After a meal at a Forces Canteen we returned to the transit camp and found it in a state of uproar. A parade was on and a roll call being taken. The Sergeant Major came along the line with his list, we had booked our seats to return to the unit, so all was well with us. Some had been in the camp for 6 weeks and had not bothered to book so they were taken out of the parade and next day sent up North to join a long range penetration unit.

On the Tuesday we reached Poona and rejoined our unit, they were having an easy time as they had no tanks and very little to do. Most of them had had malaria or were still in hospital with it. There was plenty of leisure time and I was able to play a lot of cricket and was looking forward to a cricket match against the Poona club which had been arranged but unfortunately it did not take place as we had orders to move.

The journey was to Cocanada, on the East coast, about

200 miles North of Madras. We had a special train, rather crowded and the heat was very trying, toilet facilities were very crude and our only chance of having a wash was when we stopped at a station and jumped out and found a tap.

We reached Cocanada and were taken to the Camp, a few miles away. It was the usual affair, bashas and sand everywhere.

After a few weeks our new tanks arrived, they were "DD" tanks, similar to those used in the D-Day invasion of Europe. They were fitted with tough canvas round the top of the tank and when the hollow ribs in the canvas were inflated, under pressure, you had a watertight screen round the top of the tank, about 8 feet high and this enabled the tank to keep afloat.

The drive could be switched from the tracks to two propellers at the rear and these gave you forward movement and steering when in the water.

These tanks would be taken by landing craft to within 4 miles of the enemy coast and then discharged into the sea from which distance they would be able to make their way to the shore. We were told that we would be trained and eventually used for an assault on the coast of Malaya.

I was Squadron Clerk now and did very little training but was busy with all the new drafts that were coming in and keeping up to date records of training.

We went out to a firing range for a fortnight and I was taken along to keep the records and during that time I did go out with them one day and did some firing which I enjoyed. Most days the tanks left the camp at 8am and did not return until late afternoon so I had plenty of free time.

I used to walk across the plain to some jungle about 2 miles away and catch butterflies. I had made a net from mosquito netting and had a small bottle of chloroform which one of our officers got from the MO. One morning I made the trip and was following a track just inside the jungle when it led me to an open space and there, facing me, not a dozen yards away was a wolf. It was the size of a good Alsatian. For minutes we just stared at one another, I was afraid to move towards it and thought it unwise to attempt to run away. I was unarmed, there were no stones about so I decided to move along the edge of the jungle at right angles to the wolf. This I did and to my great relief the wolf did not follow but made off for the jungle on the opposite side of the open space and there it stopped and started howling. Near this spot I found the skin which a snake had shed, it was over 10 feet long, I looked round for the snake but could not find it.

We returned to Cocanada and continued training and then we had instructions for a party of 24, mainly tank drivers, to proceed to North Burma to take over some tanks from General Stilwill's force and drive them down to Mandalay. They were to be handed over to another unit for an attack down the Burma Road to Rangoon. There were 2 officers and their batmen, Wilkinson and myself and the rest of the party were all drivers. We travelled by train to Calcutta and from there to an airfield in Comilla. The plane to carry us the rest of the journey was waiting but we found it could only take twenty so Wilkinson and myself and the two batmen were left behind with instructions to follow on when we could get a lift and join them on the Burma Road. We remained in the camp at Comilla having our meals but never going on parades. One day the Sergeant Major found us, the two batmen were put on fatigues and Wilkinson and I were sent to work in an office - they had discovered that we were both bank clerks.

We found ourselves working with one British trooper and an Indian Captain and the job was to send reinforcements to Indian Armoured Units in Burma. The trooper left after three days to join another unit so Wilkie and I had the job of deciding who to send into battle. Apart from the trade of the poor chap we had to consider his religion and caste.

The Indian captain was a very decent fellow and we did not mind working with him quite often till late at night. When we were told that we were returning to our unit the following day the captain insisted that as it was the last evening he would like us to have dinner with him. It was curried chicken, the real stuff and wine, very nice. The next morning we reported to the orderly room and saw the Colonel of the unit who said that he had tried to get us a flight to Calcutta but had not been able to manage it so it would be necessary to make the slow train and boat journey. He thanked us for what we had done and shook hands. We reached Calcutta on the following day and reported to a transit camp where they told us that they would arrange for our train journey to Cocanada. After a few days we enquired if they had been able to arrange our bookings and we were told nothing was available and they kept telling us this for three weeks so we suggested that we called at the station and saw the RTO. This we did and were told that we could go next day, in fact, we could have gone on any day during the past 3 weeks.

We got back to Cocanada the day before the party returned from Burma.

More training until June 1945 when we were told that we were moving North to the port of Vizagapatam where an invasion force was building up for the invasion of Malaya. One Squadron had moved and we were going on the following day but that evening news came through that the

Japs had surrendered and the war was over.

We were given demob groups and mine was 23. In October we were paraded and were told demob groups up to 25 were being sent home. We had a final parade and then it was discovered that 4 of us, the only ones in group 23, were not included. On enquiring we were told that if we went home with this party we would have leave for a month and then return to the Services for a fortnight, so it had been decided to hold us back. So we said goodbye to fellows we had lived with for three and a half years. One of them was a Sergeant named Leadbetter from Lancashire, he had gone out with me as a trooper and although we had never been pals we had always got on well together, he was most upset that the four of us were being left behind and we appreciated his sympathy. He told us how he was looking forward to going to his local in his uniform and wearing his Burma Star ribbon. The trucks moved off taking the party to the station but a young officer, who had been drinking with the sergeants, insisted that poor Leadbetter went with him in his Jeep. When the officer reached the station he drove on by as some kind of a joke but after some distance he decided he had gone far enough and reversed to turn round. The road was narrow and the bank sloped down to a single rail fence, the Jeep was running back and got out of control and went under the rail, the Sergeant was unable to duck and he died on the spot with a broken neck. Back in camp we did not hear of it until next day and we were very depressed. I believe there was an enquiry but never heard the result.

We remained a month, with nothing to do, just wasting time and then the day came when our papers came through. The four of us were all troopers and they put me in charge of the party. It was not an easy journey, with trains not keeping to any timetable, and often, when they did arrive, they were so crowded, both inside and on the roof that you could not get in. At one station, in the middle of the night, we had to let one train go because of this overcrowding so when the next one came in, some hours later, we made for a first class compartment, crawled through the window and lay down out of sight until we had left the station. The rest of the journey to Bombay and then on to the repatriation centre at Doulalli was made in comfort. Here we remained for several days until our papers were ready for us to get on a boat.

I was on fatigues one afternoon and helping to load officer's kit to be taken to the docks at Bombay. Some of the articles were heavy wooden chests and loading them into steel vans in the heat was hard work, we were not very gentle with them. I was amazed to come across one chest with the name Captain AGC Hodges RAMC, as a boy he had gone to school with me at Ludlow during the First World War. I knew that he had become a doctor.

A few days later we were on the boat, the Corfu, and we left India behind. We were all put on fatigues of course, my duties were to wash down the mess tables after meals, quite easy. I slept on deck until we reached Port Suez but after that we were not allowed to as the weather was getting too cold. We entered the canal and ran into a gale and by the time we reached the Bitter Lake it had got much worse. A tanker, anchored just ahead of where we were was blown right across our bows. Engines were reversed and our anchor was dropped but this did not stop a collision, we rammed the tanker amidships. She must have rolled 45 degrees but righted herself and as we backed away we saw that she had a big hole in her side, fortunately above water level and we found that we had a big hole in our bows. We carried on to Port Said and there spent a week filling in the hole with concrete. The gale continued right through the Mediterranean to Gibraltar.

Very few of the men came for meals during this period so I had an even easier time. Through the Bay of Biscay and up the English Channel. It was wonderful to see England again, everything was so green and the countryside looked so neat and tidy. We docked at Southampton after an absence of one thousand, three hundred and forty days, what a long holiday!

Time for a break.

7945642 Trooper G H Heynes
Royal Armoured Corps

About the Author

Gordon Henry Heynes was born in 1904 and raised in the village of Craven Arms in Shropshire. In his twenties his work with Lloyds bank took him to the city of Gloucester, where he settled and in 1935 married fellow bank worker Muriel Colwell.

During World War II he volunteered, joining the Royal Armoured Corps and training as a tank gunner. He was posted to first to India and then to Burma, where he saw active combat and was seriously injured in battle.

After the war he returned successfully to civilian life, raising a family and resuming his bank career.

He died in 1982, at the age of seventy-eight.

This book was prepared from Gordon Heynes' original manuscript by his grandsons, Neal and Gary Bircher.

contact@nealbircherbooks.co.uk

Facebook / Neal Bircher Author

Printed in Great Britain
by Amazon